Dog Days

by Beth Gruber

Content Adviser: Professor Peter Bower, Barnard College, Columbia University, New York, New York
Reading Adviser: Frances J. Bonacci, Reading Specialist, Cambridge, Massachusetts

COMPASS POINT BOOKS

MINNEAPOLIS, MINNESOTA

Compass Point Books
3109 West 50th Street, #115
Minneapolis, MN 55410

Visit Compass Point Books on the Internet at *www.compasspointbooks.com*
or e-mail your request to *custserv@compasspointbooks.com*

Photographs ©: Royalty-Free/Corbis, cover; Corel, 3, 5; Photos.com, 6; Corel, 7 (left); Photos.com, 7 (right);Photospin, 8;Clipart.com, 10; Photos.com,11;Clipart.com,12 (top right);Corel,12 (bottom left),13 (top left); Clipart.com, 13 (top center left), 13 (bottom left); Corel,13 (center); Photos.com,13 (bottom center left); Creatas/Creatas/PictureQuest, 15; PhotoDisc,16; Photospin,17; Photos.com,18; PhotoDisc,19 (top right); Photos.com,19 (bottom right); Ryan McVay/Getty Images,20; Photos.com, 21; Clipart.com,22 (center); Photospin, 22 (top left), 22 (bottom left),23; Clipart.com,24,25; Ingram,26 (top far left); Photos.com, 26 (top center), 26 (right center); Clipart.com, 26 (bottom left); Corbis, 27 (bottom center); Sstock/AgeFotostock, 27 (top right); Photos.com, 27 (center left), 28 (top left); Clipart.com, 28 (bottom left), 28 (center),28 (top right), 28 (bottom right); Photos.com, 28 (bottom center), 29 (top right); Clipart.com, 29 (bottom right), 31

Creative Director: Terri Foley
Managing Editor: Catherine Neitge
Editors: Sandra E. Will/Bill SMITH STUDIO and Jennifer VanVoorst
Photo Researchers: Christie Silver and Tanya Guerrero/Bill SMITH STUDIO
Designers: Brock Waldron, Ron Leighton, and Brian Kobberger/Bill SMITH STUDIO and Les Tranby
Educational Consultant: Diane Smolinski

Library of Congress Cataloging-in-Publication Data
  Gruber, Beth.
  Dog days / by Beth Gruber.
  p. cm. — (Pet's point of view)
  Includes bibliographical references (p.   ).
  ISBN 0-7565-0698-0 (hardcover)
  1. Dogs—Juvenile literature. 2. Dogs—Miscellaneous—Juvenile literature. I. Title. II. Series.
  SF426.5.G78 2004
  636.7—dc22   2004002331

Table of Contents

"From *my* point of view!"

NOTE: In this book, words that are defined in Words to Know are in **bold** the first time they appear in the text.

Who Is Your Dog?

You and Your Dog

Animal Almanac

Ruff Beginnings

When you look at a photograph of a sharp-toothed, snarling wolf, it is hard to believe that a dog like me is descended from such a ferocious beast. But I am!

Like humans and our wolf ancestors, dogs are naturally social creatures, so **domesticating** us was not difficult. In return for food and shelter, we were happy to do whatever jobs our "people" required. Our relationship goes all the way back to the Stone Age, when we trotted beside **Paleolithic** humans across the Bering Strait into the New World. For over 10,000 years, we have been used as **sentinels,** for transport, and for herding. We have come a long way from wolf to woof, but many things about us can be traced back to our wild ancestors.

The group of dogs known as sheepdogs or shepherds are so named because of their skill at herding and protecting livestock.

It's All Relative

I share my wolf ancestry with other members of my animal family, *Canidae*. Aside from wolves, my nearest relatives include coyotes, jackals, dingoes, and foxes. Look at our heads, our bodies, and the way we move—do you see the family resemblance?

My wild family has a lot in common with humans as well. Like humans, we are extremely social animals, and we live in family groups called **packs.** For domesticated dogs, though, our humans make up our pack. Although I consider my humans to be my mom and dad, my real mom was a **dam** and my father a **sire.** I have between six and 10 brothers and sisters in my **litter,** and my smallest sibling will always be the **runt** to me.

Wolf

Most of us will find new homes and families sometime after we are eight weeks old, but while we are puppies together, we play games just like our wild relatives to decide who is strongest.

Despite our common wild background, dogs come in different shapes and sizes and with different colors and coats. We are as unique as people, and yet we are all the same under the skin.

Beagle dam and litter

Domestic dog

Did You Know?

One dam, one sire, and their offspring can produce 4,373 puppies in just seven years!

The Inside Story

It is hard to imagine that a giant Great Dane, a miniature poodle, and a mid-sized **mutt** are built the same way, but we all are. My skeleton is similar to that of a human as well, although I walk on all fours. I have a heart, lungs, a brain, a stomach, intestines, and a liver. No matter my size or **breed,** I have 27 major bones, not including the bones in my tail, and strong muscles for running, chasing, and playing.

My tongue is one of my most important muscles. I use it to lap up food and water, clean my coat, and lick my owners to show affection. When I'm hot, I stick my tongue out of my mouth and make a "ha-ha-ha" sound called panting, which is the way I cool off.

Dog Years

How old am I in human years? Today, most people calculate a dog's age this way:

1st dog year = 15 human years

2nd dog year = 9 human years

3rd dog year and each year after = 4 human years

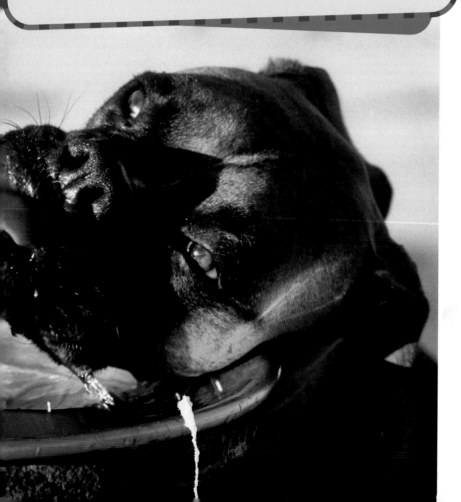

If you see me panting, make sure I have plenty of clean, cold water in my bowl and a cool place to rest. You'd want a tall glass of water and some air conditioning if you were hot, wouldn't you?

My teeth are so sharp and strong that I can chew almost anything—even shoes you forget to put away! I have 42 teeth, including six pairs of incisors and two pairs of **canine** teeth that I use to rip and bite my food. The rest of my teeth are molars. Gnawing on rawhide bones helps keep my teeth clean and healthy, but you will need to brush them often if you do not want me to have rotten teeth and bad breath.

Scent-sational

Like the wolf and other natural predators, I rely on my senses of sight, sound, and smell to navigate my world.

My sense of sight is equal to or better than a human's. I can detect even the smallest of motions. However, I do not see color. Instead, I use a combination of cues, such as texture, brightness, and position to recognize images.

My ears are extremely sensitive. Blow a whistle that does not seem to make a noise, and I will respond. My range of hearing is wider and sharper than a human's. People can hear low noises from 15 feet (4.5 meters) away, but I can hear the same noise from a distance of 75 feet (23 m)!

Dogs can rotate their ears in the direction of a sound. This ability helps them determine where the sound is coming from.

My nose has more than 20 million "smell cells"—four times more than humans—that I use to identify scents and objects around me. Notice how my nose twitches when somebody new is near. When I meet another dog, I do not shake hands like people do. Instead, I will smell its **hindquarters** to determine if it is male or female, friendly or aggressive. Unlike humans, who use their eyes to locate objects in a room, I rely more on my sense of smell to remember where my favorite places are located. Of course, I also use my nose to sniff out good things to eat, just like people do!

Dalmatians

All Kinds of Dogs

Aside from our basic anatomy, dog breeds are as different from one another as people are. There are between 400 and 500 different dog breeds, all of which are categorized by group. The non-sporting group includes breeds not listed in the chart, such as bulldogs and Dalmatians. This group was formed primarily for dog shows, and its member breeds vary in size and characteristics.

Group	Breeds	Characteristics
Sporting Dogs 	Include weimaraners, German shorthaired pointers, English setters, golden retrievers, and English springer spaniels.	• Bred for hunting, retrieving, swimming, and working all day with a human companion. • Common traits include sharp eyes, keen noses, long, hanging ears, and soft mouths. • Sporting dogs are friendly, respond well to training, make great companions, and require a great deal of exercise.

Group	Breeds	Characteristics
Working Dogs	Include rescue dogs such as the St. Bernard, guard dogs such as the Doberman pinscher, and Northern dogs such as the Samoyed.	• Guard dogs are very territorial and suspicious of people and places they don't know. • Rescue dogs are bred to find people and are much more trusting than guard dogs. • Northern dogs are friendly toward strangers but enjoy hunting small animals.
Herding Dogs	Include border collies, Great Pyrenees, and German shepherds.	• Bred to help farmers move or protect herds of livestock. • Athletic and smart. • Enjoy the company of other animals.
Terriers	Include West Highland terriers, Scotties, Airedales, and Bedlingtons.	• Bred for the purpose of catching rodents. • Powerful diggers. • Breeds vary by size, but most have wiry coats, short, upright ears, **docked** tails, and long, strong jaws.
Hounds	Include scent hounds, like the bloodhound, basset hound, and Rhodesian ridgeback, and sight hounds, like the greyhound and Saluki.	• Scent hounds track by smell. They enjoy trailing and chasing prey and will bark loudly when they catch an animal. • Sight hounds track by sight. Outdoors, they enjoy chasing small animals. Indoors, they are quiet and can be shy around other animals or strangers.
Toy Dogs	Include pugs, Maltese, Shih-Tzus, and Chihuahuas.	• Bred to be pampered companions. • Intelligent, sensitive, and can quickly learn to communicate their needs. • Enjoy attention and rewards and will quickly learn tasks to earn them.

Your Pooch Pal

Like my wolf ancestors, I am a pack animal, and my human family is my pack. The **alpha dog** in my family is usually the person who trained me when I was a puppy, disciplines me when I am naughty, and feeds me when I am hungry. I will always listen to my alpha. Even though my alpha is human, he or she is still "top dog" with me.

You might notice that I have a unique relationship with each of the people in my pack. I might be playful and affectionate with one person and gentle or protective with another. I respond to signals people send me. If you want to be my friend, hold your hand in a loose fist, extend it slowly, and let me give it a sniff. I might give it a lick or wag my tail to show you that I would like to get to know you better!

Leader of the Pack

As a natural pack animal, I always look to a leader to tell me what to do. You can be my leader by looking directly into my eyes when you talk to me, which will let me know who is in charge.

15

Give Me Love!

Raising a dog is a lot like raising a child. I thrive on love and require lots of attention, but I have special needs, too.

Just like humans, I need fresh water and food every day. I love to eat what you are eating, but dog food is better for me. Make sure to feed me the right amount for my size and breed; otherwise, I will definitely overeat!

I also need training. Training makes me feel secure because I know what is expected of me. It is important to train me when I am a puppy. There are many different styles of **obedience** training, but whichever you choose, it should be firm and consistent.

Like people, dogs appreciate regular mealtimes. It is important to establish a routine feeding schedule for your dog.

Unlike cats, who use a litter box, I need to be walked at least three times a day. If I am healthy and well-trained, I will never soil the area in which I eat or sleep, and I will get upset if I have an accident in the house.

I am not fussy, but I like to have a place that is all my own for napping during the afternoon, sleeping at night, and for quiet times when there is too much going on around me.

Some of us need special grooming. Dogs with long hair need to be brushed every day so our hair doesn't get matted, but dogs with short hair usually do not need to be brushed as often.

Make time to pet, talk, and play with me often. Exercise is a great way for us to spend time together. I like to play go-fetch and tug-of-war. I can even catch a flying disc in the air!

Canine Checklist:

▶ Do I have a collar and a tag with your name and address, in case I get lost?
▶ Do I have a regular veterinarian to give me annual **vaccines** and treat emergencies?
▶ Do I have a license? Many states require them.
▶ Do I have someone who I know and trust to look after me when you are away?

Telling Tails

Do you want to know what I'm thinking? Listen to my barks, whines, yips, and howls. Observe my facial expressions and body language. Pay close attention to my tail.

When my tail points upright and wags cautiously back and forth, I am saying "hello" and waiting to see what you will do next. A slow wag with my tail slightly lowered means that I do not know what you want me to do. Rephrase your command, and I will listen more closely. If my tail is slightly lowered and my body just a little bit tense, I am probably trying to find out about something that has gotten my attention.

How can you tell when I am happy? My tail will be loose and a bit lower than parallel to the ground. When I am not feeling well or if I am down in the dumps, I will usually hold my tail low and sway slightly. It may be time to take me for a walk or maybe even for a visit to the vet.

Watch out! If I shake slightly and hold my tail upright, I am sending you a warning that I am angry or scared and might attack. If my tail is tucked between my legs, I am telling you that I am frightened.

Did You Know?

Did you know that on average, dogs like me can understand roughly 60 words and simple phrases? Some of us can even understand up to 300!

19

My Favorite Things

What do you like to do with *your* free time? Play catch? Race down the street? Watch TV? So do I! Depending upon my breed, size, and shape, I might prefer a soft toy to a noisy one, a stick to a chew-bone, or a football to a flying disc. Perhaps I would simply like to dig a hole, or lie on a sofa and watch all the action around me.

Working dogs, like malamutes, like to dig or move sticks for play. Terriers love to chase, catch, and shake things. Greyhounds love to run at full speed. Bulldogs prefer "lazing around."

Almost any well-made toy will satisfy my natural tendency to chase, chew, or tug at an object. Rope tug toys are great for an indoor game of tug-of-war. Tossing a flying disc, ball, or throw toy is an excellent way to teach me to retrieve.

Chewable or rubber toys will keep me busy when I am left alone.

The way I play mimics the way my wolf ancestors played in the wild. I might chase a stuffed toy and tear it apart or bury a bone in a favorite place to play with later. Regardless of my breed, though, my favorite thing to play with is my best friend—and that's my owner.

Gearing Up

Caring for a dog is a big responsibility, but these items make it easier for you to keep me happy, healthy, and safe.

Collar: My collar should be soft and easy to clean. Use a nylon collar when I am a puppy, and replace it with a larger one as I grow.

Identification Tag: Dog tags are required by law in many states. They are available from your local vet and should contain contact information like a phone number that can be used if I get lost.

Leash: Leashes come in various lengths. Short leashes are best for training puppies. Longer, stronger leashes are best for larger, older, and more powerful dogs. If I tend to tug on my leash, I may prefer a harness that will not pull on my windpipe.

Bed: Dog beds come in all shapes and sizes. A beanbag bed is soft and luxurious. An open metal crate with a soft pillow or blanket inside provides a safe place for me to sleep and play when you are away from home.

Bowls: Food and water bowls can be made of hard plastic, ceramic, or stainless steel. Be sure to clean my water bowl every morning, and wash my food bowl after each meal.

Grooming Tools: A sturdy brush with wire bristles, a toothbrush, and toothpaste especially made for dogs are important grooming tools. Chicken-flavored toothpaste makes brushing my teeth a special treat!

Planetary Bow Wow

Dogs are popular throughout the world, and more than 200 million of us live with human families today. North America has the most pet dogs (68 million).

Chihuahuas are named after the state of the same name in Mexico. They were sacred to the Aztecs and were eaten in some religious ceremonies.

North America

South America

The French were equally fond of their dogs, particularly during the time of Louis XIV (1638–1715), when dogs' coats were clipped and styled to mimic the hairstyles of the day.

Records dating back more than 4,000 years show that the ancient Chinese revered dogs. The Fu Dog, or Lion Dog, was a symbol of happiness and good fortune.

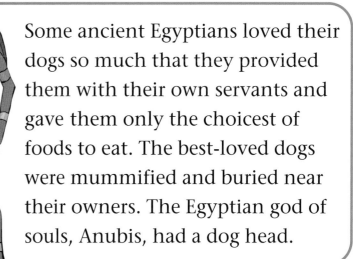

Asia

Europe

Africa

Australia

Some ancient Egyptians loved their dogs so much that they provided them with their own servants and gave them only the choicest of foods to eat. The best-loved dogs were mummified and buried near their owners. The Egyptian god of souls, Anubis, had a dog head.

Fun Facts Fur Real!

Pest Patrol!

The Yorkshire terrier was bred in the 1800s in Yorkshire, England, for the purpose of hunting and killing rats. Although the breed is quite small, its ability to pursue prey at high speeds, dig deep below the ground, and hold large objects in its powerful little jaws proved perfect for catching the pesky critters and shaking them to death.

Hot Dogs?

Dalmatians were bred as coach dogs. They ran underneath coaches to keep away other animals that might scare the horses. When fire engines were pulled by horses, Dalmatians helped ensure that the fire company arrived on the scene quickly. Dalmatians remain firehouse mascots to this day.

Bobbie's Big Adventure

In 1923, a collie named Bobbie from Oregon traveled 3,000 miles (4,800 km) over six months to get back to his owner in Illinois. When he got home, he leapt onto the bed where his master was napping and waited patiently for his owner to awaken. Good dog!

Quiet, Please!

The only dog that does not bark is the African Basenji. It is also one of the oldest dog breeds. Paintings of the Basenji were found on the tombs of Egyptian pharaohs.

Record-Breakers Dog-Gone It!

THE OLDEST DOG BREED IS THE SALUKI, which was domesticated in 329 B.C. in ancient Egypt. The Saluki were pets to Egyptian royalty.

THE WORLD'S TALLEST DOG, a Great Dane named Harvey, stands 41.5 inches (105 centimeters) high. He was measured from the ground to the top of the shoulder. Harvey is also the longest dog alive. He is 7.4 feet (2.25 m) from nose to tail-tip.

CHANDA-LEAH, A TOY POODLE from Ontario, Canada, enjoys bow-wowing audiences with a record-breaking repertoire of 469 tricks. She can play the piano, untie the knot in a shoelace, fetch a tissue if you sneeze, and even do multiplication tables for the numbers three, four, and five. In 2000, she was named the world's smartest dog by the *Guinness Book of World Records*.

A BORDER COLLIE NAMED BRAMBLE from Bridgewater, Somerset, England, lived to be 27 years old, making her the oldest dog ever recorded.

THE LONGEST DOG SWIM occurred on September 2, 1995. Two black Labradors named Kai and Gypsy swam from Lanai to Maui, Hawaii. They swam 9.5 miles (15 km) in 6 hours, 3 minutes, and 42 seconds.

IN 1993, AN 18-MONTH-OLD LERCHER dog named Stag jumped a wall that was 12 feet (4 m) tall.

THE DOG WITH THE LONGEST EARS is named Mr. Jeffries. He is an English basset hound and has ears that measure 11.5 inches (29 cm).

Important Dates Timeline

| 10000 B.C. | 350 B.C. | 1800 A.D. | 1850 | 1900 | 1950 | 2000 |

10000 B.C. Dogs are domesticated.

350 B.C. Alexander the Great is saved from a charging elephant by his dog.

1866 A.D. Henry Bergh, a philanthropist and diplomat, founds the ASPCA (American Society for the Prevention of Cruelty to Animals) in New York.

1877 The first Westminster Kennel Club Dog Show is held in New York City. It will come to be known as the Olympics of dog shows.

1884 The American Kennel Club is founded. It maintains the largest registry of **purebred** dogs in the world.

1927 Ivan Pavlov publishes ground-breaking studies on responses and reflexes based on research performed using his dog.

1931 Japanese Akitas are declared national treasures in their homeland.

1943 "Lassie Come Home," a movie starring an intelligent and brave collie, opens in theaters.

1958 A stray dog from Moscow, named Laika ("barker" in Russian), is sent into space by the Russian space program in Sputnik 5 to see if living things can survive in outer space. Laika perishes in space.

2002 **Musher** Martin Buser and his sled dogs set a record for the **Iditarod** when they complete the 1,112-mile (1,779-km) Alaskan course in eight days, 22 hours, 46 minutes, and two seconds.

Important Dogs Canine Superstars

hroughout history, dogs have helped humans in countless ways. Dogs' natural ability to read human signals has made them more than just "man's best friend." They work as service animals for the handicapped and assist firefighters and the police. Dogs are smarter than chimps when it comes to cooperating and communicating with humans. They have also been known to save their owners from much larger animals, such as bears and elephants.

9-11 Canine Hero

On September 11, 2001, an 11-year-old golden retriever named Bear was the first search-and-rescue dog to arrive on the scene following the collapse of the World Trade Center. He worked an exhausting 18 hours a day searching for survivors. In 2003, the *Guinness Book of World Records* declared Bear to be "the most celebrated dog in the world."

Rescue Dog

Barry, a St. Bernard, is perhaps the world's most heroic dog. He was born in the Swiss Alps in 1800. Over a period of 10 years, he rescued more than 2,000 travelers who found themselves trapped in the mountain pass that shares his breed's name.

Chilly Dog

When tales of great dogs are told, Balto's name tops the list. In 1925, this courageous husky led a team of sled dogs more than 1,000 miles (1,600 kilometers) from Anchorage to Nome, Alaska—in blizzard conditions—carrying **serum** to stop a dangerous **diphtheria** outbreak. His legendary journey inspired Alaska's famous Iditarod Sled Dog Race.

Words to Know

alpha dog: the leader of a pack of dogs or wolves who is responsible for their protection and guidance

breed: a dog classification similar to a human's nationality

canine: belonging to or resembling a dog

dam: the mother of a litter

diphtheria: a serious disease caused by bacteria

docked: shortened

domesticating: training an animal to live with humans

hindquarters: the rear end of a dog

Iditarod: a legendary sled dog race held annually in Alaska

litter: the puppies born at the same time from the same mother

musher: the person in command of a dogsled team

mutt: a dog that has parents of more than one breed; a mixed-breed dog

obedience: the ability and willingness to follow commands

packs: the social, not biological, families in which dogs and their canine relatives live

Paleolithic: of or relating to the Stone Age

purebred: offspring that result from the mating of two dogs with the same bloodlines and characteristics; also known as pedigreed

runt: the smallest dog in a litter

sentinels: animals or people who watch over or guard something

serum: a liquid used to prevent or cure a disease

sire: the father of a litter

vaccines: medical preparations used to kill dangerous viruses

Where To Learn More

At the Library

Fogle, Bruce, D.V.M. *The New Encyclopedia of Dogs*. New York: Dorling Kindersley, 2000.

Gerstenfeld, Sheldon L. *ASPCA Complete Guide to Dogs: Everything You Need to Know About Choosing and Caring for Your Pet*. New York: Chronicle Books, 1999.

Steiger, Brad, and Sherry Hansen Steiger. *Dog Miracles: Inspirational and Heroic True Stories*. Holbrook, Mass.: Adams Media Corporation, 2001.

Whitehead, Sarah. *Puppy Training for Kids*. New York: Barron's Educational Series, Inc., 2001.

On the Web

For more information on dogs, use FactHound to track down Web sites related to this book.

1. Go to *www.facthound.com*

2. Type in a search word related to this book or this book ID: 0756506980.

3. Click on the *Fetch It* button.

Your trusty FactHound will fetch the best Web sites for you!

On the Road

American Kennel Club's Museum of the Dog
1721 S. Mason Road
St. Louis, MO
314/821-3647
dogarts@aol.com

Santa Fe Humane Society's WestMUTTster Annual Dog Show and Picnic
Santa Fe, New Mexico
Held every June; awards given to mixed-breeds for Most Outrageous Tail, Most-Mixed Mutt, Best Trick, and Looks Most Like Owner
(Events of similar name and format occur in almost every state. Contact your local humane society.)

Westminster Kennel Club's Annual Dog Show
Madison Square Garden, New York, New York
Held every February; awards given to pure-breeds for Best in Group and Best in Show (televised)

INDEX

ABOUT THE AUTHOR

Beth Gruber has worked in children's publishing for almost 20 years as an author, editor, and reviewer of many books for young readers. She also interviews other authors and TV show creators who write for children. Beth is a graduate of the NYU School of Journalism. Her passions are writing and reading. She lives in New York City with her 15-year-old Yorkshire terrier named Kozo.